W9-AUD-633

How *Cats*
Made It to
the Stage

Peg Robinson

Cavendish
Square

New York

Published in 2019 by Cavendish Square Publishing, LLC
243 5th Avenue, Suite 136, New York, NY 10016
Copyright © 2019 by Cavendish Square Publishing, LLC

First Edition

Library of Congress Cataloging-in-Publication Data

Names: Robinson, Peg, author.
Title: How Cats made it to the stage / Peg Robinson.
Description: New York : Cavendish Square, 2018. | Series: Getting to Broadway | Includes bibliographical references and index.
Identifiers: LCCN 2017050600 (print) | LCCN 2017053964 (ebook) | ISBN 9781502635037 (ebook) | ISBN 9781502635020 (library bound) | ISBN 9781502635044 (pbk.)
Subjects: LCSH: Lloyd Webber, Andrew, 1948- Cats--Juvenile literature.
Classification: LCC ML3930.L58 (ebook) | LCC ML3930.L58 R63 2018 (print) | DDC 792.6/42--dc23
LC record available at https://lccn.loc.gov/2017050600

Editorial Director: David McNamara
Editor: Tracey Maciejewski
Copy Editor: Rebecca Rohan
Associate Art Director: Amy Greenan
Designer: Lindsey Auten
Production Coordinator: Karol Szymczuk
Photo Research: J8 Media

The photographs in this book are used by permission and through the courtesy of: Cover Ted Thai/The LIFE Picture Collection/Getty Images; p. 4 C Wenn/Photos/Newscom; p. 7 Ed Bailey/AP Images; p. 9 George Douglas/Picture Post/Getty Images; p. 10 Jonathan Wiggs/The Boston Globe/Getty Images; p. 11 Paul Fearn/Alamy Stock Photo; p. 12 Daily Express /Hulton Archive/Getty Images; p. 21 Popperfoto/Getty Images; p. 22 Don Arnold/WireImage/Getty Images; p. 27 David Goddard/Getty Images; p. 29 Anthony Harvey/Getty Images; p. 30 Bruce Glikas/FilmMagic/Getty Images; p. 31 Baron/Hulton Archive/Getty Images; p. 33 Aaron Showalter/Sipa USA/Newscom; p. 35 United News/Popperfoto/Getty Images; p. 39 Mark Cuthbert/UK Press/Getty Images; p. 41 Richard Lewis/ AP Images; p. 44 Jenny Anderson/WireImage/Getty Images; p. 48 PA Images/Getty Images; p. 51 Ann Rosener/Pix Inc./The LIFE Images Collection/Getty Images; p. 52 PA Images/Alamy Stock Photo; p. 57 JTB/Media Creation/Inc./Alamy Stock Photo; p. 59 Richard Drew/AP Images; p. 70 Robbie Jack/Corbis/Getty Images.

Printed in the United States of America

Contents

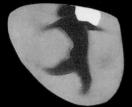
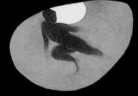

CATS

MUSIC BY ANDREW LLOYD WEBBER
BASED ON 'OLD POSSUM'S BOOK OF PRACTICAL CATS' BY T. S. ELIOT

PRESENTED BY   CAMERON MACKINTOSH,   THE REALLY USEFUL COMPANY
LIMITED,   DAVID GEFFEN   AND   THE SHUBERT ORGANIZATION

THE "CATS" COMPANY: (IN ALPHABETICAL ORDER)
KENNETH ARD,   BETTY BUCKLEY,   RENÉ CEBALLOS,   WALTER CHARLES,
RENÉ CLEMENTE,   MARLÈNE DANIELLE,   WENDY EDMEAD,   DIANE
FRATANTONI,   STEVEN GELFER,   HARRY GROENER,   STEVEN HACK,
STEPHEN HANAN,   ROBERT HOSHOUR,   JANET L. HUBERT,   REED JONES,
WHITNEY KERSHAW,   DONNA KING,   CHRISTINE LANGNER,   TERRENCE V.
MANN,   ANNA McNEELY,   HECTOR JAIME MERCADO,   BOB MORRISEY,
CYNTHIA ONRUBIA,   KEN PAGE,   SUSAN POWERS,   CAROL RICHARDS,   JOEL
ROBERTSON,   TIMOTHY SCOTT,   HERMAN W. SEBEK,   BONNIE SIMMONS

EXECUTIVE PRODUCERS   R. TYLER GATCHELL, JR.,   PETER NEUFELD,
ORCHESTRATIONS BY DAVID CULLEN   AND   ANDREW LLOYD WEBBER,
PRODUCTION MUSICAL DIRECTOR   STANLEY LEBOWSKY,   MUSICAL
DIRECTOR RENE WIEGERT,   SOUND DESIGN BY **MARTIN LEVAN**,   LIGHTING
DESIGN BY **DAVID HERSEY**,   DESIGNED BY **JOHN NAPIER**,   ASSOCIATE
DIRECTOR AND CHOREOGRAPHER **GILLIAN LYNNE**,   DIRECTED BY **TREVOR NUNN**.

ORIGINAL CAST ALBUM ON GEFFEN RECORDS & TAPES ⊖
🐾 **WINTER GARDEN THEATRE**

Chapter 1

Cats

The night was October 7, 1982. The place was the Winter Garden Theatre, on Broadway, in New York City. The show was *Cats*, based on T.S. Eliot's *Old Possum's Book of Practical Cats*. The audience anticipated a good night. The show, which had opened in London a year before, had received mixed reviews but had sold tons of tickets and thrilled audiences. The music was by composer Andrew Lloyd Webber, who had conceived of the show. The choreographer was Gillian Lynne. Some of the song lyrics, including the now-classic song "Memory," were written by director Trevor Nunn, but the majority of the show consisted of Eliot's own well-loved verses set to music.

Where It All Begins

The house lights went dark. The overture began. It was stirring and complex. The stage lights rose, and the set was revealed in dim light—an alley under street lamps. Then,

Opposite: Original poster advertising the first Broadway production of *Cats*

prowling to the restless music, the cats came out, slim and agile, fat and lazy, young and old. Their clever faces were each distinct. The audience was already falling under the spell, as Munkustrap, the primary narrator, and the other cats sang:

> **Are you blind when you're born?**
> **Can you see in the dark?**
> **Can you look at a king?**
> **Would you sit on his throne?**

The old theater magic came to life.

The rest of the night was history. At the time it finally closed production, *Cats* had become the longest-running show ever to have appeared on Broadway, with a total of 6,138 performances. Even now it remains the fourth–longest running show. It has been seen worldwide in off-Broadway productions—productions of all sorts, from high school shows to fully professional touring companies. The London stage production was videotaped live in 1998. It was revived in London in 2014 and opened again on Broadway in 2016. It remains a landmark show in the history of theater.

However, the show didn't really start that night. It started years earlier, when Andrew Lloyd Webber decided to try to change the way he created music. He had composed music for shows before, including *Jesus Christ Superstar* and *Evita*. Lyricists then wrote the words to go with Lloyd Webber's melodies. He wanted to see if he could work in

Tony-award winner John Napier, costume designer for *Cats*

reverse by writing melodies to go with words that were already set down.

Creative artists must push themselves to grow. There's territory where no teacher can take you, so artists invent their own homework. They set themselves challenges and stretch their skills farther and farther. They want to be excellent, and they invent ways to get better. Webber, who wanted to compose better, invented a homework project for himself.

He had been familiar with T.S. Eliot's book *Old Possum's Book of Practical Cats* since he was a boy. He loved the clever, funny poems, and the characters of the different cats and their stories. He decided to try to write music to accompany the poems.

That is where *Cats* really began: with T.S. Eliot and *Old Possum's Book of Practical Cats*.

T.S. Eliot

The musical *Cats* opened in London, moved on to Broadway, and has been around the world on tour. It has been performed by hundreds of small theater companies—high schools, colleges, local theater clubs, small semi-pro groups—all of which brought the show to life. But the story of *Cats* always starts with T.S. Eliot and his book of nonsense poetry.

Who was Eliot? Many people who love *Cats* know nothing more about Eliot than that he wrote the poems on which the show is based. Many don't even know he was famous long before the musical opened in London.

T.S. Eliot, the author of *Old Possum's Book of Practical Cats*

Summer home of T.S. Eliot's family, in Gloucester, MA

Eliot defies categories. He is both American and English, a serious poet as well as a comic master. His first marriage was so unhappy that some people assumed Eliot was homosexual; yet his second marriage, to a woman nearly forty years his junior, was so successful and so sensual as to throw former theories out the window.

Thomas Stearns Eliot was born on September 26, 1888, in Saint Louis, Missouri. His family had its origins in Boston, Massachusetts. His grandfather, a minister in the Unitarian Christian church, moved west to Saint Louis in the early 1800s to open a church in the city and raised his family there; however, the Eliots kept their cultural and family ties to Massachusetts. Eliot was educated in traditional boarding schools in the Northeast. After getting a degree and doing post-graduate work at Harvard, in Cambridge, Massachusetts, he went to Europe, eventually ending up in England at the University of Oxford prior to World War II.

He married Vivienne Haigh-Wood soon after the war broke out. The marriage was unhappy. Haigh-Wood was emotionally unstable, and they came to dislike each other. However, her desire to remain in her native country during wartime strengthened Eliot's own affection for England. Eventually, they separated but never divorced. Haigh-Wood's brother had her committed to a mental hospital in 1938, and she was still a resident in one at the time of her death, in 1947.

Vivienne Haigh-Wood, T.S. Eliot's first wife

Eliot would remain single until 1957, when he married his secretary, Valerie Fletcher. Fletcher, while younger by forty years, was a lifelong fan of Eliot's. She had sought contact years previously and had worked with Eliot for eight years prior to their marriage. Fletcher played a crucial role

T.S. Eliot and his second wife, Valerie Eliot

in the development of *Cats*. After Eliot's death, she served as his literary executor. She had control over how his works were used, and her choice to let Andrew Lloyd Webber use *Old Possum's Book of Practical Cats*, and the limits she placed on that use, made a huge difference in the final form of the musical.

T.S. Eliot is now seen as both an American writer and an English writer. He was a great poet—he won the 1948 Nobel Prize for literature. His poetry remains among the most popular, enduring, and influential work in English. He was also a playwright, an essayist, and a theological writer. In all his serious writing, he was best known for themes of religion, morality, and the meaning of life. And then there was his comic poetry, which brought us *Cats*.

Old Possum's Book of Practical Cats

It is hard to decide whether T.S. Eliot is more famous for his serious writing or for his one outstanding collection of comic poetry. He is one of the most influential voices in modern poetry. Works like "The Waste Land," "Four Quartets," and "The Love Song of J. Alfred Prufrock" are considered necessary subjects of study for those who want to understand the shift from Victorian poetry to modern poetry. However, his comic poetry was beloved even before Andrew Lloyd Webber wrote and produced *Cats*. Since the musical opened and proved a hit, millions and millions of people have come to know Eliot's work through the music and dancing of the play. In the end, thanks to the theater, Eliot may end up equally famous for both his serious and his comic work.

Old Possum's Book of Practical Cats is a collection of comic poems written for T.S. Eliot's child-associates—for his godchildren and for the children of friends. Eliot had no children of his own. He enjoyed visiting with children, though. He treated them as part of his extended family. He sent them greetings and special messages through his correspondence with their parents and produced poetry meant to amuse them. All but two songs used in *Cats* are drawn from the published collection he wrote to amuse these young friends.

The play is based firmly in the book, and in Eliot's other work. Valerie Fletcher Eliot, his widow and literary executor, insisted on that. She was very protective of her husband's work. Her decision that Lloyd Webber could only use Eliot's poems forced the play to take a very different form than that of other plays of the time. However, her contribution of unpublished work of Eliot's, and her understanding of Eliot's intentions when he was writing, also changed the play. Valerie's contributions provided the show with a theme and a plot. Without that, it would always have been a concert, but not a play. It was Valerie who showed Lloyd Webber that her husband had not only wanted to entertain and delight children, he also had a story he originally had hoped to tell.

Eliot began writing *Old Possum's Book of Practical Cats* during the years 1934 and 1935. The children who were given poems included Tom Faber, the son of his partner at Faber & Faber publishing, and his goddaughter Alison Tandy, who was the daughter of Eliot's friends Geoffrey and Doris Tandy. Other poems were sent to the adults in the family, including Doris, better known as "Polly."

The Eliot estate has copies of some of the letters exchanged between Eliot and the Tandys. These letters include early drafts and suggestions of the poems that eventually were published as *Old Possum's Book of Practical Cats*. Some of these letters can be seen through the British Library website (https://www.bl.uk/20th-century-literature/articles/an-introduction-to-old-possums-book-of-practical-cats).

Eliot was also discussing the poems with his fellow editors at Faber & Faber. This information was included in the material Valerie Fletcher was able to show Lloyd Webber.

Eliot originally intended a larger book, with two parts that were eventually left out. Originally, he intended a series of dog poems to go with the cat poems, including poems describing the warring relationship between the dogs and the cats. He thought he would frame the story of the cats and dogs fighting with a story of a man in white spats who moves through this world of dogs and cats, and eventually resolves the story by rising up into a higher plane called the Heavyside Layer.

Long discussions later, Eliot and his friends decided that the book should be simply about cats. They also decided that it would be aimed at a children's audience, and that one cat poem he'd already been working on was too serious for the audience. As a result, the book published was very different from the book originally imagined. Valerie's contributions pushed Lloyd Webber and his team to make their play more like Eliot's original idea in some ways.

The 1939 collection contained fourteen poems. A fifteenth ("Captain Morgan Introduces Himself") was added in a later edition in 1952. The musical, *Cats*, contains portions of all the original fourteen, plus material drawn from drafts, notes, and fragments from related writings by Eliot, and provided by Eliot's widow, Valerie. The connection between the original poems and the versions used in the musical are clear and unmistakable. Valerie Eliot was only willing to give Andrew Lloyd Webber and his team the rights to create the musical on the condition that the core of the work consisted of Eliot's writing.

The originals differ slightly from the stage play, though. The words are almost unchanged; Valerie Eliot made sure of that. But those first fourteen poems do not form a stable story line. Each poem is freestanding. Lloyd Webber and his team, with active help from Valerie Eliot, had to develop a story and

THE IMPORTANCE OF OLD POSSUM'S BOOK OF PRACTICAL CATS

Old Possum's Book of Practical Cats was first published on October 5, 1939, after more than eight years in development. Faber & Faber put out an initial run of 3,005 books, respectable but not huge. It could have been a terrible flop: Eliot was better known for serious poetry and prose on mature topics. The new book was intended for an entirely different audience—children, and adults in search of light poetry. Where much of Eliot's work was weighty and somber, evoking deep moral and religious themes, and tackling the fears and uncertainty of an unsettled period of history, *Old Possum's Book of Practical Cats* was sheer fun.

Faber & Faber were lucky. The book sold well from the first run, a huge hit, and it also proved to be a steady classic. It was bought and read, given to friends and to children, and kept not simply as a curious thing T.S. Eliot had written, but because people loved it. The sales manager at Faber & Faber said at the time, "*Cats* are giving general satisfaction." Reviews were overall positive, with Kirkus Reviews opining, "One can't say much for the kind of feline society Mr. Eliot keeps, but his verses are very entertaining and smack a bit of Archie and Mehitabel, of Gilbert and of Lewis Carroll. Written with gusto and humor." (November 16, 1939)

The book was never a major title but remained an evergreen children's classic. The collection was sufficiently popular to be put out in an entirely new edition in 1953, at which time an additional poem, "Captain Morgan Introduces Himself," was added. Over the decades between its first publication and the opening of *Cats*, it was produced in multiple editions—illustrated and otherwise, paperback and hardback, with minor edits and alteration by Eliot over the years. From a publisher's point of view, it was a solid winner, selling enough books over a long-enough period to more than pay back the investments made in both the original print run and later runs and editions.

The original book was loved specifically as comic, light writing. The original fourteen poems and the additional fifteenth, added in 1953, had been selected specifically to suit a niche audience. Some pieces that would be used or referred to within the musical *Cats*, such as the one about Grizabella, the glamour cat, were left out because they would not fit an audience looking for light, humorous reading. "Grizabella" was thought to be too sad for this audience. Other poems were left out because the book came to be seen as very specifically about cats. An entire set of poems relating to dogs was removed, with only the poem about the battle of the Pekes and the Poms remaining because the hero of the piece is a cat.

Those who bought and loved the book at the time did so because they loved it just as it was: a book of funny cat poems by one of the most skilled poets of the age. There were other light poets during the period who were equally loved. Ogden Nash was immensely popular at the time, a genius at producing light verse; similarly,

Dorothy Parker and Stevie Smith were treasured for their sharp wit and biting verses. Edward Lear and Lewis Carroll, of the generations preceding Eliot, were still loved and cherished. Winnie-the-Pooh's author, A.A. Milne, was as well known for his light poetry for adults and children as for his prose for either age group. It was a time and period that supported and enjoyed comic poets, when readers expected high quality from their comic writers.

Since the opening of *Cats*, sales of the book have become even stronger. The show helps publicize the book; the book helps prepare young audiences for the show. Together, both are cherished by a fond audience.

theme to knit the poems together as a consistent stage show. They also had to make minor alterations to the original poetry to increase the dramatic effect of the material. The end result is a collaborative effort, but an effort built entirely on Eliot's own writing, and Eliot's own thoughts and artistic vision. The result is so much Eliot's own work that, when *Cats* won the Tony Award for best book for a musical, the award was given in Eliot's name. Valerie Eliot accepted the award for her late husband. She had succeeded. His words, no one else's, were the heart and soul of the musical *Cats*.

It is common today to think of *Cats* as an Andrew Lloyd Webber production, and to give credit to the team he collected when creating the show. It remains important,

T.S. ELIOT'S HONORS

Cats is the only theatrical musical written by a Nobel Prize–winning author.

though, to remember that the original work was that of T.S. Eliot. He created a classic collection of children's poetry, and his wife and Lloyd Webber's team used that, and elements of his other work, to translate that classic to the stage. Eliot's serious poetry continues to be appreciated and admired. The original collection, *Old Possum's Book of Practical Cats*, is still loved and read around the world. Finally, *Cats*, the inspired transformation of his poems, is famous world 'round, with no sign of that fame ending for generations to come. It is a classic of the musical theater.

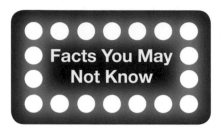

A Cat Person

It was no accident T.S. Eliot wrote a book about cats, rather than about dogs, or horses, or parakeets, or ferrets. The author was a cat lover, and over the years, he owned and enjoyed many cats of his own. He also enjoyed meeting and visiting with other people's cats. He took special delight in talking about cats with friends and with children, just for the fun of it.

It is easy to see how playful Eliot was when you read his letters about cats and the poems in his collection. His letters overflow with cats—cats mentioned in passing, cats that appear to be people he and Doris "Polly" Tandy both knew, cats in poems. His letters include rough drafts of poems that later appeared in the collection and drafts of poems he later decided did not belong. He shared the cats he wrote about with laughter, but also with the trust of a writer showing his work to a discerning reader. It is clear he

Valerie Eliot and Andrew Lloyd Webber shared a love of cats.

wanted to both amuse and impress his readers—especially Polly Tandy and her daughter Alison.

The poem titled "The Naming of Cats" clearly reflected his own ideas and preferences. Indeed, one of his own cats makes an appearance in the list of possible names he offers for cats: Eliot did own a cat named "Jellylorum." He was fond of unusual names for cats, and his pets included one named Wiscus and another named George Pushdragon.

Chapter 2

The Journey to the Stage

Cats is obviously very closely related to *Old Possum's Book of Practical Cats*. There are only two songs in the show that are not drawn directly from the published book. There are no songs not intimately tied to Eliot's writing, drawing on his words, his images, and his ideas. Yet there are real and powerful differences between the two works of art. A musical stage show is not a small book of published comic verse. It's worth taking the time to think about how the two differ, before going on to see how *Cats* was developed from the original material Eliot wrote.

Cats is a performance piece. It's intended to be performed by dancers, singers, and actors, in front of a live audience. Everything about the show has been arranged to give the audience a great experience. The *Cats* experience is almost entirely unlike the experience of reading Eliot's book.

Opposite: Grizabella the Glamour Cat, played by Delta Goodrem in a Sydney, Australia production of *Cats*

To begin with, Eliot's writing was not intended to be a showstopper. Where *Cats* is big and loud and showy, Eliot's book is quiet and controlled and humorous on a much less exciting level. If you were a fanboy or fangirl crazy for the book, you'd be unhappy with the play, because the entire personality of the show is different from the personality of the book it's based on. The change in style alone is huge.

Unlike the book, *Cats* tells a story. It's not the story Eliot imagined, of the man in white spats who walks through the peculiar and amusing world of the jellicle cats and pollicle dogs, only to rise up into the Heavyside Layer. Instead, it's the story of a community of cats throwing a Jellicle Ball at which they will decide what cat—what one special, singular cat—will go to the Heavyside Layer to be reborn. It's the story of Grizabella, the former glamour cat, who has fallen into age and hard times and loneliness. Grizabella, the outcast of the cat community. It's the story of Old Deuteronomy, who rules the cats and organizes their actions and who will decide which cat is reborn. Within that it's a story of the entire community coming together to party—and then to listen to each other, and think, and consider who is to be reborn.

That story does not exist in *Old Possum's Book of Practical Cats*. It's only hinted at in bits and pieces of what Valerie Fletcher showed Andrew Lloyd Webber. It's a story that Lloyd Webber and his team pieced together.

The story is told by actors, who take Eliot's words and add in acting and singing and dancing. They act out relationships that do not even exist in the book. In the book, each cat poem exists on its own, describing a cat or

a group of cats, an idea about cats, a story about a cat …
but the cats don't come out of their poems and interact.
They don't hiss at Grizabella and try to force her out of the
community. The older cats do not mother the younger ones.
There is no beautiful, silent White Cat to dance a graceful,
heartbreaking, and beautiful solo.

The themes of love and loss, of tenderness and caring,
of sharing a world with all the other cats—they're not in the
original book, but they're in the play. Eliot might well have
approved of them, but he didn't add them into his book.

The musical still has Eliot's words at its heart. Valerie
Fletcher Eliot made certain of that. But it grew far beyond
the words alone, picking up a story and a theme of age and
loss and hope and happiness along the way. It became an
in-your-face, butt-kicking, spectacular show, instead of a
quietly funny little book.

Valerie Fletcher Eliot might have chosen to stop it—it
changed so much even without changing a word of what
Eliot wrote. She didn't. But, then, she knew T.S. Eliot loved
the theater. He had written for the theater. He'd had shows
produced. She knew he understood that a work changes on
the way from the page to the stage. She let *Cats* become what
it was, though what it was differed so much from the book.
As a result, *Cats* went on to win fans and readers for her late
husband's poetry it would never have had without the musical.

The Idea

These days, almost anyone who loves musical theater has
heard of Andrew Lloyd Webber. In 1977, though, when Lloyd

Webber first thought of putting the words of *Old Possum's Book of Practical Cats* to music, he was still a comparatively young, if successful, theatrical composer. His first success, *Joseph and the Amazing Technicolor Dream Coat*, written in collaboration with Tim Rice as his lyricist, had been a hit in London's West End—the rough equivalent of a Broadway hit in the United States. Since then, Lloyd Webber had been lucky. He and Rice had produced *Jesus Christ Superstar* to great acclaim, and in 1978, *Evita* had taken off.

Lloyd Webber had had an amazing beginning to his career but no specific idea what he wanted to do next. He only knew he wanted to continue to stretch his skills and grow as a composer. In his work with Tim Rice, the two had developed a pattern. Lloyd Webber would write music. Rice would then fit lyrics to the music. Lloyd Webber thought it would be interesting to see if he could reverse that pattern and write music for existing words. Looking for poems he thought would be interesting, he chose four pieces from *Old Possum's Book of Practical Cats*. He was familiar with the book from his childhood, and he felt the structures and rhythms would fit musical theater while challenging him to come up with equally creative music. In 1977 and 1978, he began writing settings to some of the poems from Eliot's collection. He had no particular intention of going beyond that.

Other projects to stretch his skills also occupied him. One, a one-woman show called *Tell Me on a Sunday*, had not originally been intended for theater production. In 1980, it was presented on television. Its success made Lloyd Webber rethink his other works in progress. He thought his settings for Eliot's poems might be suited as concert

Sydmonton Estate, location of Andrew Lloyd Webber's Sydmonton Festival

performance pieces. He chose four settings and presented them at the 1980 Sydmonton Festival, an event organized and held on his property, in an old former chapel.

That was when luck and serendipity struck. He chose to invite Valerie Eliot. He knew that Valerie was Eliot's literary executor and was known for being extremely protective of how her late husband's writing was used. Lloyd Webber knew that if he was ever to do more with his project, he would need her permission, if not her personal interest.

That night, Valerie liked what she heard. She felt that her late husband, who loved theater, would have been thrilled to have his light poetry translated into theater. She also had access to related material that she thought might contribute to Lloyd Webber's understanding of T.S. Eliot's poems. She approached Lloyd Webber with old typescripts of her husband's work. One of those pieces included a fragment called "Grizabella." It was the poem that had been left out of the original collection, as Eliot had felt it was too sad for a children's book of light verse.

That bit of sad poetry, though, was the seed from which the musical *Cats* grew.

The Team and the Story

When Lloyd Webber read the material Valerie Eliot brought to him, he decided that the music he had been working on might be a dramatic musical, instead of a collection of free-standing concert pieces. There is a difference between the two. While a collection of concert pieces may be unified by author, theme, and material, there is usually no central dramatic story arc, and no expectation of a dramatic, theatrical presentation. Concert material is performed as music first, with theater as a secondary concern.

A musical show, though, has come to mean something different. While there is room in musical theater for "revues," which are collections of music, dance, and comic skits, even revues are expected to be dramatic, staged presentations. They include music, dancing, acting, costume, and more. A full musical, though, is unified even beyond that: a true musical is a story. Like opera, it's a dramatic

The creative team of *Cats*: director Trevor Nunn (*left*), composer Andrew Lloyd Webber (*center*), and choreographer Gillian Lynne (*right*), with cats from the cast

presentation of a short story. Characters in a musical each play a role in telling a story the audience cares about.

Lloyd Webber knew that if he was going to change direction and turn his concert compositions into a musical score, he needed help. The typescript of "Grizabella" had given him an idea of what story he wanted to tell. But he needed a team to work with. In 1980, he began to assemble a team to help develop a new theatrical musical based on Eliot's collection of comic poems for children.

He knew he would be facing some serious challenges. To begin with, Valerie Eliot was determined that any show

Andrew Lloyd Webber on the red carpet for the revival of *Cats* on Broadway in 2016

would be based almost exclusively on T.S. Eliot's own words. The team would not be allowed to rethink the poems and rewrite them extensively. While Lloyd Webber would need someone to help add a few new pieces to provide connections and bridges between the poems, he could not offer a chance to rewrite the poetry. He'd have to find a skilled partner who would be happy to find a story within the poems, and provide the small bits of original material that would help the audience follow along. The partner's ego would have to take a back seat to Eliot's words.

Further, because of those limits, the choreography would be a major element in the storytelling. Lloyd Webber had to find a brilliant choreographer he could count on to bring *Cats* to life.

The Choreographer

Lloyd Webber began searching for team members when he started discussions with the successful West End producer

Gillian Lynne as a young ballerina

Cameron Mackintosh. He trusted Mackintosh to help him find the talent he needed to turn a series of poems into a serious hit musical. *Cats*, unlike most plays, tells its story with no spoken lines. *Cats* is performed, rather than being told. That meant Lloyd Webber needed team members who were great artists and great storytellers.

The movement of the actors and the dancing make a big difference to the show. If the words of the show are freestanding poems, the movement is similar to one big ballet. The cats interact, showing the audience what they think, how they feel, what they want and hope and fear. The story is in their actions more than their words. Choosing a choreographer who could tell stories with dancers was very important.

Lloyd Webber also knew he wanted to include some of the flavor of the London dance world in any production he might make of *Cats*. After considering the choices open to him, he decided to meet with Gillian Lynne.

Gillian Lynne's professional career started when she was sixteen, in 1942. She began her career as a dancer. She was a soloist in the Sadler's Wells Ballet Company. Trained in both ballet and jazz dance, she eventually began working as a choreographer as well as a star dancer, with choreographic credits as early as *Puss in Boots* in 1962. She worked successfully as a director and a choreographer for many years; however, *Cats* would serve as her first real breakout work, bringing her serious recognition for the first time and winning her a Tony nomination.

Cats is considered by many to be a dance show above all else; Gillian Lynne's contributions to the show as choreographer were irreplaceable. It was her understanding

Gillian Lynne at the curtain call for the 10,000th Broadway performance of *Cats*

The Journey to the Stage **33**

of character and story, and her ability to apply her years of knowledge to the challenges of the show, which turned *Cats* into a dramatic presentation. Her choices influenced every aspect of the show. Her work with the performers helped define characters, influenced costume, controlled the pacing and dynamic of the acts, and served as the focus of interest at any given moment.

Choreography is seldom praised as highly as it ought to be. Because it is pure motion, writers can struggle to describe the full effect great choreography contributes to a production. This is true of Lynne's work on *Cats*. If Eliot wrote the original poems, and Lloyd Webber and Trevor Nunn wove together the story itself, Gillian Lynne created the style, the sizzle, and the world of *Cats*.

She also provided one crucial contact. It was through Gillian Lynne that Lloyd Webber came to choose Trevor Nunn, who had worked with Lynne previously. Her recommendation gave Andrew Lloyd Webber the working partner he needed to construct the story of Grizabella and the trip through memory to the Heavyside Layer.

The Director

Lloyd Webber approached Trevor Nunn, a theater director with a professional career going back to his 1964 entry into the Royal Shakespeare Company. Nunn turned out to be a perfect choice of collaborator. He was a director who enjoyed the process of solving problems and working out ways to communicate the story of a play. Being asked to collaborate on the creation of a story was right up his alley.

Cats director Trevor Nunn in 1982

Lloyd Webber and Nunn discussed the poems in *Old Possum's Book of Practical Cats*. Lloyd Webber then showed Nunn the fragment of poetry called "Grizabella." This was the poem that Valerie Eliot had brought to Lloyd Webber on the night of the Sydmonton Festival—the poem that had been left out of Eliot's comic collection on purpose, because it was too sad.

That fragment of poem, one verse long, presented the cat Grizabella, a female cat living as an outcast—fallen on hard times, abandoned. Those who see her and recognize her find it amazing she is even alive still, and struggle to imagine her as she once was: Grizabella, the Glamour Cat. That one verse tells a story of fallen stars, lost dreams, aged divas, and lives that last longer than happiness.

All Eliot's other poems were in some sense happy poems about proud, fulfilled animals leading productive lives—or remembering those lives in the contentment of their old age. Grizabella, though, is a cat in need of a happy ending. She's a cat people can care about, and root for. She's a cat who needs something.

That kind of need provides the engine that drives a dramatic storyline. Lloyd Webber and Nunn found themselves agreeing, and their opinion was supported by Valerie Eliot: Grizabella's story could provide the foundation on which to build a dramatic musical.

Nunn and Lloyd Webber also found elements of their story in further material provided by Valerie. In a letter T.S. Eliot wrote describing some of his earlier ideas for how the collection of poems would be structured, he said:

> The idea of the volume was to have different poems on appropriate subjects … recited by the Man in White Spats … At the end they all go up in a balloon, self, Spats, and dogs and cats.
>
> Up up up past the Russell Hotel,
>
> Up up up to the Heaviside Layer.

Lloyd Webber and Nunn read T.S. Eliot's poetry. They read essays of his. They discussed his thoughts and beliefs and the themes of his writing. They discussed his own original idea of a collection of poems with just enough story to have a resolution of the characters rising and rising to a mysterious Heavyside Layer.

Lloyd Webber and Nunn decided that it would not be wrong to see the Heavyside Layer as a heaven—or a reincarnation. T.S. Eliot had begun his life as a Unitarian Christian. For many years, he had been a student of both Hinduism and Buddhism. He ultimately became a very strong, committed Anglican. His writing was full of metaphors for the afterlife and suggestions of heaven and reincarnation.

Now they had Grizabella, a cat who needed a happy ending, and a heavenly resolution that T.S. Eliot himself had once imagined. The ending, with its hints of death and reincarnation, was suited to the feline subjects of the other poems—after all, cats have nine lives! What better answer for a cat that has come to the end of one life, than to move on to a new life?

As the two men worked, they picked out themes from the many poems they were reading. They came to realize that they had a story, and a theme, and a development arc, but that none of the poems they were using stated clearly what the central issue was: recovering happiness. Grizabella needed her happy ending.

In searching for writing by Eliot that would express their main theme, Lloyd Webber and Nunn found a passage from one of Eliot's most famous—and serious—poems. They selected a quote from the "Dry Salvages" section of the poem group "Little Gidding." The quote discusses the nature of true happiness, and how happiness reveals truth beyond time. The writing hints at eternity and emptiness. The two writers chose to use that as their anchor to their newfound themes and the nature of their story. By then, the outline of the story was set. Lloyd Webber made minor modifications on Eliot's "The Song of the Jellicles" to introduce the key idea of an annual ball followed by the choice of a single cat to ascend to the Heavyside Layer for reincarnation. The Jellicle Ball celebration would take up the first act of the show. The second act would focus on a search for a cat to be sent to the Heavyside Layer to receive a new life. The many cats Eliot wrote of in his poems would be the characters in the two acts, and their poems would provide the songs and stories. As a final unifying piece, Trevor Nunn wrote one original song, intentionally drawing from T.S. Eliot's "Preludes" and "Rhapsody on a Windy Night."

By then, Lloyd Webber and Nunn knew they had what they needed for a great show. It was time to bring in other team members and to look for investors.

Unfortunately, there were few people interested in backing the show. Cameron Mackintosh, the producer, and Andrew Lloyd Webber were struggling to find interested

Trevor Nunn at a memorial service for Sir David Frost in 2014

VALERIE ELIOT

Valerie Eliot is perhaps the most influential person to have been involved in bringing *Cats* to the stage, after the obvious team members are accounted for. Few people recognize the depth of her contribution to the show, or to her husband's literary legacy.

T.S. Eliot married badly in his twenties, to Vivienne Haigh-Wood. The match was misery for both, yet both held to the standards of the time, remaining married for Haigh-Wood's lifetime rather than divorcing. The couple formally separated in 1933. Vivienne was committed to a psychiatric hospital by her brother in 1938. She died in 1947.

During the years of the separation, Eliot had at least two platonic sweethearts: a former girlfriend, Emily Hale, who was close to him during the time he taught at Harvard; and Mary Trevelyan, an Englishwoman. After Vivienne's death, it's thought that Trevelyan had hopes Eliot would marry her; however, he did not, living for many years alone.

Then, in 1957, when Eliot was sixty-eight, he married Valerie Fletcher, who was only thirty. Fletcher had been a fan of Eliot's poetry for years and had been thrilled to obtain an introduction to Eliot, and to eventually gain a post as his secretary, a role she served in for eight years before her marriage. The two remained happily married until Eliot's death, in 1965.

Valerie was Eliot's chosen literary executor. In that role, she was devoted, intelligent, and capable. She protected his literary legacy, guarding who was given rights to use Eliot's writing, and how it was used, while working to ensure his works and his letters would be published.

Her decision to allow Andrew Lloyd Webber to first develop a set of concert compositions based on the work was actually a very rare privilege. Valerie Eliot was determined to defend her late

Valerie Eliot appears at a 2004 ceremony honoring poet Ezra Pound, a friend of T.S. Eliot's.

husband's work from trivial use. She allowed no official biography. She wanted to be sure his writing and letters were available to the public before scholars tried to put their own spin on them. She was very cautious in allowing artists to quote Eliot's work. However, she gave Lloyd Webber the permission he needed to create something unique.

She helped shape what he created, too. Her offerings of select material taken from her archives of Eliot's writing, plus her contribution of thought and consideration, shaped the work. Her biggest contribution was a limit—the limit on material not by Eliot himself. She was determined that the show must hold tight to Eliot's own writing. She didn't want the words to deviate much from Eliot's own words.

She could have destroyed the show, if she'd been less willing to accept change. Instead, she allowed just enough change, understanding that original works like "Memory" were necessary to help tie the final story together. Her knowledge of Eliot's writing, of theater, and of publishing, allowed her to make brilliant choices about how far she would permit Lloyd Webber and his team to deviate from Eliot's own work. She recognized what details had to change, to allow Eliot's own spirit to shine through. It is unlikely that Lloyd Webber, or any other artists, would have accomplished anything as pure, and as brilliant, without someone like Valerie Eliot maintaining the limits she imposed. While Lloyd Webber gives Valerie Eliot credit for much of what she contributed, neither he nor others often recognize her vital role in shaping and guiding Lloyd Webber's final vision of T.S. Eliot's work.

"angels" (investors). Lloyd Webber even took out a mortgage on his own home to support the work. In the end, the two almost reinvented show financing. They drew on dozens of small investors, each contributing as little as £750 apiece, approximately $1,750 in today's money.

Creating a Show

During his prior years of theatrical work, Andrew Lloyd Webber had begun building his own production company. His team now began to work with this core group, bringing in other performers and specialists as necessary to develop the final version of the show.

A DARK-HORSE ENTRY
At the time of its opening, almost no one thought *Cats* would be a success, much less the brilliant success it proved to be.

The production, which opened in the New London Theater, was developed to be performed "in the round." John Napier was selected as the designer, and he created the key visual look of the production, including set design, costume design, and makeup design. He knew what he wanted to create for the show: "A world for cats that would not only achieve a greater degree of intimacy with the audience than is possible in most conventional theatres but would also point up the humor of the show and its occasional wackiness." David

This promotional shot from the original production of *Cats* shows the varied looks of the cats onstage.

Hersey was the lighting designer, producing a lighting plan that made good use of the challenging theater-in-the-round staging of the show. The conductor, Harry Rabinowicz, was ready to lead an orchestra that included several synthesizers.

SIR ANDREW

Andrew Lloyd Webber was knighted in 1992. In 1997, he was further granted a lifetime peerage. He is currently titled Baron Lloyd-Webber and can be addressed as The Right Honorable The Lord Lloyd-Webber. Because of the rules of punctuation of the peerage in England, his formal title is hyphenated (Lloyd-Webber), though the hyphen is not used in the ordinary use of his professional name.

Opening

The show opened on May 11, 1981, at the New London Theater. From the start, it was a hit. It ran continually in the West End from its opening until its twenty-first anniversary, on May 11, 2002, for a total of 8,949 performances.

In 1982, it opened on Broadway, where it was similarly successful. For nine years, from 1997 to 2006, it was the longest-running show on Broadway. In 2006, it was surpassed by *The Phantom of the Opera*, another Andrew Lloyd Webber production. It remains the fourth–longest running Broadway play.

THE SYDMONTON FESTIVAL

Reading about the development of *Cats*, it is easy to be confused by mentions of the Sydmonton Festival. Even articles on Andrew Lloyd Webber do not always make it clear that he started the festival, that it's held on his property, or that it's intended as a way of trying out new and exploratory work in front of an audience with strong theater and arts connections. That lack of clarity can change how people understand what happened with *Cats*.

As an artist, one of the most difficult challenges in theater is that of finding an audience that can provide useful reactions. Reviewers and critics are often too busy trying to decide if a work matches their idea of what something should be. General audiences often are trapped by the fact that they "don't know much about art, but they know what they like." They know what they like, but not why. They don't always know why they don't like something, either. It's hard to find out what you need to know from an average audience. An audience that understands art a bit, and understands the professional art world, can tell you things you need to know.

In 1975, Andrew Lloyd Webber established the Sydmonton Festival, a summer arts festival held in a deconsecrated church on his estate. The festival's purpose was to provide a place for artists to perform their work in front of a "private audience of people from theater, television, and film in order to gauge the future potential of the works." It was a chance for artists—including Lloyd Webber himself—to show works in progress and see what entertainment-oriented people thought about them.

An artist could not pay to get that kind of insight. Andrew Lloyd Webber didn't pay for it, either. He sold his idea as an arts festival, and people paid him for the privilege of coming to see what he and his fellow artists were working on.

Thus, it becomes more obvious why Andrew Lloyd Webber chose to perform an experiment in composing at an arts festival. It also becomes obvious why he invited Valerie Fletcher Eliot. At a private event known for trial performances, he could introduce his work without offending her as Eliot's literary executor—and if he was lucky, she'd be interested in what he was doing.

Lloyd Webber was being very clever, professionally, and it paid off. Valerie Fletcher Eliot was very interested, and thanks to that interest, Lloyd Webber eventually was able to write and produce *Cats*. Without the Sydmonton Festival, it might never have happened.

Chapter 3

West End and Broadway: *Cats* in Production

The story of *Cats'* run is a tale of two productions— the West End production and the Broadway production. Each faced different challenges and contributed to the legend of the show. Each became a historic landmark in the history of modern musical theater.

At the time *Cats* opened in the West End, in 1981, it was common for people to claim that musical theater was dead. In spite of hits, including Andrew Lloyd Webber's previous successes, musical theater was finding it difficult to transition from the Golden Age works of the early- to mid-1900s, to the age of rock music. *Cats* opened to an audience inclined to doubt the worth of modern musical theater. For

Opposite: Elaine Page backstage at the New London Theatre preview of *Cats*

the show to succeed, it had to offer excellence and a new vision of musical theater.

Cats was the prototype—the original draft—of what later came to be called a "megamusical." It was bold and extravagant. It was not limited by the neat, crisp formula that had defined Golden Age musicals. The story was powerful, and real, but sketchy at best. The focus was on the music, the dancing, and the spectacle. It combined many of the advantages of a revue, as the numbers were big, and to some extent freestanding, but its unifying story held together better than a revue. The narrative allowed for tight timing between numbers. The nature of the story, without lines or obvious skits and scenes, was fluid. The material was superb, and the performers who presented it were, also.

New London Theater

The West End production was the first, and it defined the show. It was performed in the New London Theatre, which had opened in 1973. The theater was distinctive. It had been designed in the style of Walter Gropius's Total Theater, a brilliant, innovative design Gropius created in 1927, which unfortunately was never built. The theater had been intended to provide a flexible, easily varied performance space, offering staging areas that included traditional proscenium stage arrangements and thrust stages, three-quarter round platform presentation, and a full theater-in-the-round configuration. Entire sections of the building were designed to turn and spin, changing the arrangement of seating and staging. It was like a theater crossed with a *Transformer* robot.

Architect Walter Gropius's stage design was pivotal to the success of productions like *Cats*.

The Kitten Cat, played by eleven-year-old Jessica Hill at the New
London Theatre

The New London Theater is not as extravagant as the Gropius design. It is a variable-presentation building. It was set up for a full theater-in-the-round experience for the opening of *Cats*. Theater-in-the-round places the performance area at the center of the seating space, with the audience surrounding the actors. Theater-in-the-round is a very challenging arrangement. A show like *Cats*, with many performers in action at all times, can hope to command the theater. Lesser shows can be overwhelmed. The lack of wings and staging areas places a heavy burden on technical production. A show has to offer a brilliant experience no matter what seat you are in. Anything less, and the show can fall apart, broken by its own staging.

Cats was ready to meet the challenge. Lloyd Webber and his production team had selected a brilliant cast. The performers included known stars like Brian Blessed, who appeared as both Bustopher Jones the Club Cat and as Old Deuteronomy, and new faces, including Sarah Brightman, who got her start playing Jemima, the young kitten who first accepts Grizabella, and who reprises "Memory" at the climax of the show. One superb casting choice, however, fell through in the weeks prior to opening.

Judi Dench (now Dame Judi Dench) had been cast as the show's Grizabella. Her casting was a draw for many of the other actors, overcoming reservations about the peculiar new musical, which seemed a bit ill-defined to many in the theater world at the time. She was dedicated, and excited about the show, unlike many who saw an odd, rather formless revue based on nonsense poems about cats, originally aimed at a child audience. Unfortunately, in what seemed an all-around catastrophe, she suffered a ruptured Achilles tendon before the preview performance. There are conflicting stories regarding when the injury occurred, ranging from reports of it happening a mere ten days before the first preview, to others that suggest the injury occurred before the composition of "Memory," well before the final stages of production. Regardless, it was a crippling injury, and there was no real chance Dench could recover from it in time for the opening.

Lloyd Webber and his team hurried to find a reliable replacement. Lloyd Webber had worked previously with Elaine Paige, who had starred in the title role as Eva Peron in Lloyd Webber's *Evita!* Paige was able to learn the part within the time available. The role proved to be historic for her, strengthening an already promising career.

Paige's performance wasn't the only concern that opening night. In the middle of the show, a bomb scare cleared the theater—but not before *Cats* had won its audience over.

People had come in with serious doubts. Many had expected a cute, kitsch pantomime, barely fit for children. Those who knew the challenge of theater-in-the-round had reason to feel even more fear: even a good play can be difficult in a circular theater. The show could have been dreadful, and many believed it would be.

Instead, the challenges brought out the best in the show. The scanty plot, shaved down to a bare minimum, provided just enough frame for the music and the dancing. The dancers used the full space of the theater well, exploding into the performance area from all directions, moving into and out of focus at speed. The lack of dialogue kept the pacing of the numbers tight. The quality of Eliot's original poems forced care and attention from the performers.

The set was novel; the costumes used new fabrics and ingenuity to meld feline and human elements dramatically but convincingly. The makeup helped sell the illusion of the human alley cats. The music was complex and eclectic—not so unfamiliar as to make the audience uncomfortable, but surprising in its combinations, and clever in the ways the music supported the lyrics. The choreography Gillian Lynne had developed showed off the skill of the dancers and told a story with movement that could not be told in words thanks to Valerie Eliot's rules regarding the content of the book.

It was a winner. It was bright, loud, and spectacular. It did the one thing all good theater must: it entertained.

The Winter Garden Theatre

It was another year before *Cats* would open on Broadway. The controlling team was the same as that which developed the show for the New London Theatre. Cameron MacKintosh produced, Lloyd Webber, Nunn, and Lynne served as composer/musical director, director, and assistant director/choreographer. John Napier designed the set, costumes, and makeup. The cast was new, with Betty Buckley playing Grizabella; Ken Page as Old Deuteronomy; Steven Hanan as Bustopher Jones, Growltiger, and Gus the Theater Cat; and Carol Richards as the kitten Jemima, among other outstanding performers. The cast never became as iconic as the original London cast, but it was strong and effective and ready to impress the New York theater community.

Broadway's Winter Garden Theatre is a very different performance space than the New London Theatre. It was designed traditionally, with a proscenium arch, a modest thrust stage, and an orchestra pit at the foot of the stage. If the performance area of the New London Theatre was infinitely changeable and experimental, and the theater-in-the-round configuration used in London unusual and exciting, the stage of the Winter Garden verged on dull. It forced the team to reconsider their staging. They had to work to find a way to create as explosive and immersive a show in the Winter Garden as they had in the New London.

The first choice they made was to convert the theater to the greatest degree they could. They extended the thrust stage far out into the audience seating, building a new performance platform out over the orchestra pit. John Napier transformed the entire space dramatically, extending set dressing out into the house, and extending the performance space into the audience. It was not theater-in-the-round, but it came as close as an old warhorse of a proscenium theater could hope to. The deep thrust stage altered the sight lines and wrapped the audience seating around the stage itself. Napier lowered the ceiling, too.

The environment of the New London Theatre was naturally alien to much of the audience. The environment of the Winter Garden was made alien through an act of creative imagination. As Frank Rich commented in his *New York Times* review of the opening night, "Well before the lights go down, one feels as if one has entered a mysterious spaceship on a journey through the stars to a cloud-streaked moon."

The Winter Garden production of *Cats* cemented the reputation of the show as being an immersive experience, half spectacle, half vision. Critics argued that the plot

The Winter Garden Theatre, home to the original run of *Cats* on Broadway

was thin, the music derivative, the dancing too gymnastic, the costumes too gaudy—but all admitted the audience's experience of the show was overwhelming. Those familiar with both the London production and the New York production commented on the increased intensity of the New York show. The costumes were even more dramatic. The dancing and singing were more intense, and the choreography was more explosive. The pace was relentless. The experience was intended to sweep away all before it.

The decision to play big was probably a good choice. Where the opening in London had been a complete surprise, in New York it came behind stampedes of rumor and previous reporting. *Cats* was not an unknown product in New York. Theatergoers were eagerly awaiting its success.

The show was already breaking rules by opening in New York so soon after opening in London, with the run in the New London Theatre far from over. The project still inspired disbelief, and its success in London had only underlined the sense of stunned surprise and annoyance. The year since the London opening had given theater lovers time to consider the show's weaknesses, and there was a sour-grapes sense that no matter how supersized the show, and how overwhelming the experience, the underlying quality of the show did not warrant its outsized victory. Very little but an overwhelming, oversized, amazing production could have overcome determined skepticism and judgment.

As it was, the show was as emotionally satisfying as its London sibling. Big and bold, with an inspired new set, with choreography to suit the new space, with upgraded costuming and tech, it was a winner. *Variety*'s 1982 review

Betty Buckley performed as Grizabella at the 37th Annual Tony Awards.

started with the statement, "*Cats* isn't a great musical but it's a great show and an ironclad smash." You could argue with that point, but it's an important one. Compared with the classic musicals of the Golden Age, *Cats* is a flawed creation. However, it is a brilliant show. It may not be a great example of old-style musical theater, but it's an inspired example of what came to be called a megamusical. It changed the musical form into something new, fresh, and profitable at a time when the old forms were failing to draw audiences.

Landmark Success

Cats was a record-breaker from the start. A hit against all odds, it proved that a new style and form of musical had a place in Western theater. For a time it held a special place in the world—with *Cats* already a hit in two cities, Lloyd Webber and his team soon moved further. They sent their show out with touring companies while it was still running in London and New York, turning the show into a global hit. In many ways, it is impossible to talk about the show in terms of a single production, or single run, or even in terms of a single location. *Cats* changed history by changing the entire notion of theater. By the time Lloyd Webber and his team were done, a show was no longer a local, regional production. It was an ever-moving, accessible franchise, with mobile productions you might watch in Tokyo, New York, Los Angeles, and Paris. They discovered that their franchise shows did not reduce the number of people willing to pay premium prices to see *Cats* on Broadway, or in the West End. The touring shows only acted as publicity. People fell in love with a production that had come to their hometown. Once they fell in love, they wanted to see the show in London or in New York City—the famous theater districts of the world.

Critical Response

Both the London production of *Cats* at the New London Theatre and the New York City production at the Winter

Garden Theatre got mixed reviews. Some reviewers loved it—but plenty hated it.

The show in both forms was too different from the expectations of the critics. The ways the show was great were not likely to impress reviewers much, and this isn't unusual. Most changes in the world come when someone sees something in one setting, and realizes it could be improved in another setting. But those trained to evaluate art, or design, or any other creative form, are trained to distrust new, strange styles and influences. Instead, they look for the best of what is already "normal." Critics did not like jazz music when it became popular. They laughed at rock and roll. They thought first the movies, and then television, were bad art when they were mainly new art.

Cats was new art, but many critics didn't see it. They saw a strange production in which adults dressed in slinky, silly cat suits with cat makeup and in which the dancing resembled a Vegas revue more than a proper Broadway or West End musical. A musical aimed at the common man— using the comic poems of a Nobel Prize–winning serious poet. It was loud, it seemed a bit childish, and it was strange. The plot, though it did exist, was thin—hardly even there. It was hard for the first reviewers to see it through the eyes of the ordinary audience member, who came and was swept away for a few hours, taken to a fantasy world of dancing and music and laughter and tears.

A fairly typical review of the New York production on the negative side came from critic Douglas Watt, in the *New York Daily News:*

FACTS BOX

London Opening:
May 11, 1981

Theater:
New London Theatre

Run: 8,949 performances

London Closing:
May 11, 2002 (twenty-first anniversary)
Held the title as longest running show in London
for four years, until beaten by *Les Misérables*.

Grossed: £592.3 million

New York Opening:
October 7, 1982

Theater:
Winter Garden Theatre

Run: 7,485 performances

New York Closing:
January 9, 2006
Held the title as longest running Broadway show for
nine years, until beaten by *The Phantom of the Opera*.

Grossed: $407.7 million

The razzle-dazzle of "Cats," a British cat cantata set in a junkyard that swept into the Winter Garden last night glittering like a few hundred Christmas trees, may be enough to keep you in your seat for two-and-a-half hours, if not exactly on the edge of it. But in spite of some effective moments, it makes for a strained and eventually wearing evening … "Cats" is as showy a show as one could wish for, and it is already eagerly sought after by a musical-hungry public. Yet the feeling is inescapable that it is an overblown piece of theater.

T.S. ELIOT'S OWN CATS

"Quaxo" is one of the special names offered for cats in the poem "The Naming of Cats." T.S. Eliot actually did name one of his own cats "Quaxo."

A more positive review came from *Variety*. They saw more clearly what the strengths and weaknesses of the show were, starting with the perceptive comment, "Cats isn't a great musical, but it's a great show and an ironclad smash." The entertainment paper recognized the difference between a great show and a great musical. To reviewers, a "great musical" had to meet certain clear standards in form, style, and structure. A strong plot, for example, would have been nice. But a great show only has to meet one standard, no matter how it does it—it has to delight its audience. What *Cats* lacked in elegant and refined musical structure and style, it made up for with wham-bam excitement, holding

● MEMORY ●

"Memory" is the big, showstopper song in *Cats*. It was also among the last written.

Andrew Lloyd Webber and Trevor Nunn had spent the majority of their time working on the original poetry provided by T.S. Eliot. They had planted the elements of the plot in the mild revisions they had made to Eliot's "The Song of the Jellicle Cats," which appeared as "Jellicle Songs for Jellicle Cats," and "Invitation to the Jellicle Ball." They had extended those elements using the material drawn from "The Dry Salvages," which appeared in Old Deuteronomy's solo "The Moments of Happiness," at the beginning of the second act.

As they approached opening night, though, they concluded that the show lacked a showstopper and could not do without one. They had already used the poems from *Old Possum's Book of Practical Cats* with the exception of the late addition from the 1953 edition, "Captain Morgan Introduces Himself," which was felt to share too much in common with "Growltiger's Last Stand" to be added.

Lloyd Webber used a melody he had originally begun working on for a prior project—a modernization of *La Bohème.* The project had never gone anywhere, but the melody remained. Webber refined it, working it into a complex and emotionally charged ballad form. At that point, it had no words. He brought the piece in, and Trevor Nunn approved.

Nunn then wrote words for the piece, combining images, metaphors, and phrasing from other works of T.S. Eliot. He was determined to match the emotional spirit of Grizabella's story. Together, the music and words were intended to generate a one-two punch, providing the blockbuster song the show needed.

Their work proved to be a winner. Within weeks of opening, singers were recording covers of the song. It's been a hit for many, including Elaine Paige, who originally sang the piece, and Barbra Strelsand.

"Memory" does not match the tone and texture of the other songs in *Cats*. Unlike the other songs, its words are not rooted in Eliot's own poetry in quite the same way. The music was written before the words, and the words are a pastiche that tries to summarize a show—and a poet's own emotional weight. "Memory" doesn't quite fit. Yet that may be what makes it a blockbuster. It stands out.

Eliot's words, taken from Eliot's works, blended with both Lloyd Webber and Nunn's thoughts and feelings about the poet and about the story they had created. The opposing goals, to write a hit song, yet respect Valerie Eliot's rules, forced them to express what they felt most powerfully about the story they'd created in collaboration with the great poet and his widow. The result is special: beautiful, haunting, and remarkable, it remains in the memory of all who see the show.

its audiences entranced and sending them out into the city singing afterward.

The show had never had strong support or understanding from the gatekeepers of the press. "Everybody in the West End thought we were completely and utterly crazy," Lloyd Webber says now, chuckling. "The moment that *Cats* came on stage could have been one of the most ridiculed moments in the history of theatre."

The truth is, *Cats* never had reliable support from reviewers, though it's easy enough to cherry-pick reviews to provide flattering statements by the dozen. Its audiences are another matter entirely. From the beginning, both productions had strong enough attendance to overcome the doubts of the movers and shakers of Broadway and the West End. The show was loved, even if it was not admired, by theater's elite judges. Most of all, it made money.

Money seldom impresses reviewers much. In their own minds, they often feel that mere popularity says nothing about quality or high standards. Money, however, does impress the producers and the backers of theatrical productions. It impresses directors and choreographers and designers. It impresses actors. It impresses professionals who must earn their living based on whether a show is loved or not. A brilliant work of art that audiences do not love will close in weeks, if not days. A less artistic work that the audiences adore can run for years, as *Cats* has. When that happens, actors can pay their rent, dancers can afford to go home to visit their parents, theater investors see their bank accounts grow, and producers see money rolling in that will not only pay for one show, but will then support other shows. Money makes careers. Money keeps the theaters open.

Facts You May Not Know

THE POWER OF SUCCESS
As of September 2017, the musical has had an economic impact of at least $3.2 billion on New York City alone.

So *Cats* was loved, first by the audiences who saw it, and second by the professionals who realized it was going to help keep musical theater in business. To this day, reviewers point out the weaknesses in Lloyd Webber's score. They grumble at the odd nature of the source material. They insist that the show's structure is weak, its premise a bit silly, and its nature too cute. In the end, the reviewers have lost the war. Someday *Cats* will fall out of fashion and end up a mere landmark in theater history. Its flaws are real, and time will eventually bring it down, as it brings down all but a very few works of genius.

It will still have succeeded. It pleased its creators, pleased its audiences, and pleased its investors. It made its mark. It fed a lot of actors and dancers and singers. It continues to make a lot of people very happy, and it changed theater in the process. In the face of that kind of victory, there's nothing the reviewers can say that really matters.

In 2013, *Cats* was the fourth most–profitable show in history, after *The Phantom of the Opera*, *The Lion King*, and *Wicked*. At that time, it was estimated to have made over $2 billion in gross revenues. The show is in constant production somewhere in the world and has recently been successfully revived in both New York and London. It is difficult to determine its current total gross revenues.

DESIGNING *CATS*

The primary designer of *Cats* was John Napier. He produced the stage and set designs, the props, the costumes, and the makeup for both the London and New York productions, as well as for the touring groups. He was also the principal designer on the recent revivals in London and in New York City. In many ways, John Napier controlled every major aspect of what the musical looks like and how the audience experiences the show. Napier is the artist who decided how to stage the show. He designed the set pieces and the props that occupy the stage. He designed the flexible cat costumes, so reminiscent of both dance leotards and the costumes of comic-book superheroes and supervillains. He designed the facial makeup for the primary cat characters. He even contributed to the cat's-eye design of the promotional poster logo.

Most of the millions of people who have seen *Cats* have been influenced by Napier's work. The fantasy world they step into is Napier's world, his design on all levels.

While the musical theater has always been a bit closer to fantasy than most stage drama, very little of Golden Age design comes close to the level of fantasy *Cats* demanded.

Napier was born in London, educated at the Central School of Art and Design, specializing in theater design. It was at this school he was told by one instructor that he was no good at theater design—that he was an artist, but had no talent in the field of theater.

The instructor suggested he leave. He did so, going to work at a construction site. Weeks later, he was contacted by Ralph Koltai, the head of the department, asking why Napier wasn't attending classes. He explained he'd been told to leave—and Koltai promptly ordered him to come back.

He worked in the theater for many years, slowly rising in his profession, but *Cats* was his biggest break. He knew that the theater community was laughing at Lloyd Webber's project. A show about kitty-cats didn't sound like much of a show, unless you were doing a Christmas pantomime or something similarly cute and childish.

Napier wanted something grittier and less sweet. His first inspiration was the stage set—the now-iconic garbage heap in which the characters play and prowl. He saw an alley on his drive home, and from there imagined an entire world a feral cat might live in. He designed oversized props for the cats to play with, including an old toothpaste tube. Flashing reflective glass eyes were embedded in the set to catch the light and gleam as the lighting came up.

Napier created an entire world. He went on to design the cats themselves, working to ensure the dancers would be able to move and work with Gillian Lynne's choreography, while still giving the impression of being cats. Wild, feral cats. Street cats.

He created a world apart, a cat's world, that the audience entered into. The style now has a name: it's called immersive design. John Napier, in designing the set, costumes, and makeup for *Cats*, helped bring an entirely new approach to theater design into the world.

Chapter 4

How *Cats* Made History

O ther landmark shows change society, or create new techniques for producing a show, or introduce themes that have never been considered from modern perspectives. They may introduce new actors, new writers, new composers, and new lyricists. While you could argue that *Cats* did all these things to some extent, it is most remarkable for changing what people expected of musical theater on all levels. In the process of bringing the show to the world, Andrew Lloyd Webber, his production company, and his creative team changed almost every aspect of musical theater production.

Reimagining Musicals

Lloyd Webber changed how people thought a musical should look and sound. Golden Age musicals followed

Opposite: The iconic faces of *Cats*

familiar formulas. There were simple, strong stories, often built around romances. There were expected types of songs, and reliable dance numbers. The characters were people. Fantasy and imagination tended to be contained and clearly identified. The sources might be arty and obscure, but the final musicals seldom were. The Golden Age musical's roots were in light opera and comic theater, with plenty of dialogue to move the plot and tie the show together.

Cats was different from the beginning. It grew out of a project first intended to expand the composer's own skills. It drew from an artistic tradition of classical concert music. Lloyd Webber's first vision was of a concert song cycle. His first performance was of four concert pieces performed at a music festival held on his own property. He drew from the work of the greatest literary poet of the century—and T.S. Eliot's *Old Possum's Book of Practical Cats* was accessible comic verse, which only underlined the unusual nature of what Webber was doing. He started out with the kind of art that would usually be considered elite, refined, of no great commercial value—but even at the beginning, Lloyd Webber was blending the elite with the populist, the refined and the easily accessed.

The framing story was weak—barely enough to tie the drama together. There was no dialogue. The characters were cats. The show was all fantasy and imagination. There was no clear formula. There was no love story.

All these things meant that, from the very start, *Cats* was not much like a Golden Age musical. That was part of why it was so hard to raise funds to support the show. Most investors had a hard time imagining the show could ever be anything but a failure.

Cats changed the form people expected from musical theater. Previously the two major forms common in musical theater had been the Golden Age show and the revue. Golden Age shows were straightforward light opera. The stories were formulaic, accessible, and strongly plotted. Revues were plot-free or offered only a faint pretext of a plot to tie the variety of performances together, making thin excuses for collections of song, dance, and comic skits. *Cats* drew from a different tradition, offering a high-speed spectacle. It had a stronger plot than a revue and a weaker plot than a Golden Age musical, but it offered a unified tidal wave of performance, sweeping the audience away. The show was more like the circus or a Las Vegas extravaganza than it was like previous musical theater presented in the West End or on Broadway. Shows that contain song, dance, and skits are also commonly called variety shows.

How We Do Business

Cats also changed how the business of musical theater worked. To begin with, the show was financed using many small-scale investors, rather than large-scale "angels" providing heaps of money. It expanded the range of ways a show could be financed.

It also changed the old expectations of how many productions of a show would be running at any given time, and where. Previously, an original show was treated as a one-off: it was unique for a long period of time, seldom running in multiple cities at once. The home city—the city where a show opened—had a monopoly on the show until the first run ended and the show closed. Only then was it common for a show to move to another city, or to go on tour. This is still how most theater is produced. The focus is on individual interpretation on the part of the director and performers.

So, while many people may have seen *Hamlet*, and many productions of *Hamlet* may be running at the same time, they are not all considered the same show. Instead, you go to the theater to see a director's version or a particular actor performing a role. Each is different and unique. Kenneth Brannagh's Hamlet is not the same as Benedict Cumberbatch's Hamlet, and neither of them is like Laurence Olivier. When people talk about this type of unique production, they don't say, "Have you seen *Henry V*?" They say, "Have you seen Tom Hiddleston's Henry V?"

Cameron Mackintosh and Andrew Lloyd Webber had a different idea, though. An audience could see *Cats* in London, and New York, and on tour, and while each production might differ, each would also be reliably the same.

The megamusical's shock-and-awe experience was the product. This drew the importance away from the director and the actors and the specific designers and moved the importance to the brand name of the show itself. The shift changed the nature of the product. Instead of being promoted as a unique experience, it was promoted as a reliable experience, like a movie, not a play. When you go to most plays, you look for a unique experience. When you go to a movie, though, you want to see a reliable product. People ask if you've seen *Fantastic Beasts and Where to Find Them*. They don't ask if you've seen Eddie Redmayne's *Fantastic Beasts*, even if they love Eddie Redmayne.

This was a new approach to promoting a theatrical production. It opened up the range of possibilities for making money. It would not have worked with a different style of production. Only the big-experience fireworks of a megamusical would have carried the first effort to franchise an original new work. However, that kind of experience tied to previous franchise productions: touring shows like the Ice Capades were marketed as franchise experiences. Vegas revues were and are similarly marketed as "experience" shows, even though they are not touring shows. The modern Cirque du Soleil entertainment company has gained a similar, franchise-based reputation.

Other shows, including Lloyd Webber's own *Jesus Christ Superstar*, had attempted similar franchising, to lesser success. The original impulse was a response to growing global pirating. It seemed better to franchise through licensed touring companies than to lose money to theatrical pirates overseas. In an interview prior to the opening of the recent New York City revival of *Cats*, Lloyd Webber said, "I remember back in 1971, when Robert Stigwood was my manager, Robert sat me down and said, 'We have to get *Jesus Christ Superstar* around the world now, and we have to do it quickly.' He said, 'People are going to pirate it, and there's nothing we can really do, so we must get our own productions up.'"

Careers

Cats offered many professionals their first big break—or their breakthrough. When you consider the longevity of the show in both London and New York, the touring companies, and the recent revivals, it's no wonder many people look back at the show as a landmark in their professional lives.

Obviously, Andrew Lloyd Webber should be among the first counted in that regard. Until *Cats*, he had no real blockbuster hit to his name. The albums of *Jesus Christ Superstar* and *Evita* strongly outperformed the actual productions. Nothing else he had done approached those in popularity and prestige. His career was a success, but on a small scale. *Cats*, soon followed by *Starlight Express* (a commercial hit, if not a critical favorite), and then *The Phantom of the Opera*, established Lloyd Webber as one of the premier figures of the modern international theater world.

Gillian Lynne, already an admired professional, could also count *Cats* as her career breakthrough, though for no clear reason she never received the kind of acclaim for her choreography that Webber got for his music, Trevor Nunn got for his directing, and Napier got for his set, costume, and makeup designs. Many consider this a great injustice. Lynne almost single-handedly invented a new style of choreography intended for the spectacle of the megamusical—and for a form of theater in which dance was as much part of the storytelling as were words and song. Her dancers worked at the same level as ballet dancers, giving performances that included acting and acrobatics blended into intense dance routines. Until her work, there had been nothing quite like it.

Fortunately, her genius was remembered, even if it was not properly honored with awards and public acclaim. An already respectable career blossomed after *Cats*. Later, she went on to choreograph *The Phantom of the Opera* for Lloyd Webber.

Sarah Brightman, whose career moved away from pure theater, got her start as Jemima in the original London production of *Cats*. Married to Lloyd Webber for six years in the 1990s, she also originated the role of Christine in both the London and New York versions of his show *The Phantom of the Opera*. The New York original gave a start to Rob Marshall, now better known for such accomplishments as directing the movie version of *Chicago*.

Wash, Rinse, Repeat

In 2014, *Cats* came back to London, opening for a limited run at the Palladium Theater. In 2016, it returned to New York City's Winter Garden Theatre, then went back on tour. Andrew Lloyd Webber seemed determined to prove that the success of the show in the early 1980s was no mistake.

Expectations were no higher than they had been the first time around. If anything, time and success had added a layer of cynicism to the waiting critics. Over a period of thirty-plus years, Andrew Lloyd Webber's work had been nitpicked for every possible flaw. Critics had been given

Longest Running Musicals in London (current as of 2017)

1. *Les Misérables*, 1985–present
2. *The Phantom of the Opera*, 1986–present
3. *Blood Brothers*, 1988–2012
4. *Cats*, 1981–2002
5. *Mamma Mia!* 1999–present
6. *Disney's The Lion King*, 1999–present
7. *Starlight Express*, 1984–2001
8. *Chicago*, 1997–2012
9. *Buddy – The Buddy Holly Story*, 1989–2003
10. *We Will Rock You*, 2002–2014

years in multiple venues to analyze every moment the show had to offer. The style of the megamusical had come—and was beginning to go. And yet, here came the old shock-and-awe, ready to try the old theater magic one more time.

Critical responses were mixed, as they had been for the original openings. Audience responses, though, were as positive as ever. Both productions, and the tours, have been financial winners. Further, a new, proper film of the show

CREATIVE FINANCE

So few people thought *Cats* would be a success that the producer, Cameron Mackintosh, and Lloyd Webber were struggling to raise sufficient money to cover the costs of production. In the end, they did so using a very early form of **"cloud funding,"** raising the money through small donations from interested parties. Some of the investments were as little as £750.

is planned. Universal Studios expects the movie to go into production sometime during 2018.

Evergreen

Why does a show that is regularly criticized as being nearly plot-free, predictable, loud, gaudy, and sentimental win, and win, and win again? Why do so many people love a show so many critics treat like fast food: probably good for the economy, but not very impressive?

Facts You May Not Know

SET DESIGN INSPIRATION

As mentioned earlier, John Napier's junkyard set was inspired after he drove past a junkyard at night and wondered what it would look like from a cat's perspective. It was this inspiration that led to one of the hallmark images of the show—the "levitating" tire Old Deuteronomy uses as his throne and dais. Napier created over 2,500 oversized props and set pieces to create the set and props for the dancers and actors to perform with.

Sarah Crompton, a professional theater critic, proposed a likely explanation in a 2002 article in the *Telegraph*. She compared Andrew Lloyd Webber to Paul McCartney of the Beatles, in the ancient game of Lennon vs. McCartney (and also Harrison). Of the two great composers, McCartney was always the popularizer. He was the showman. He knew what audiences liked. He knew the kind of music that would cut directly to the hearts of his audience. Lennon and Harrison were the smart ones. Their music was challenging. It took some work to understand.

McCartney made it look easy, and listeners never realized that it was far from easy. McCartney was as willing to innovate as Lennon and Harrison. He challenged forms, he played with styles, and he opened the doors of his music to a world of influence. He just never made the audience pay the cost to understand it. Instead, he was sufficiently skilled to help them understand.

He made it look easy because it was fun, and popular, and it didn't give listeners headaches, and no one had to be stoned to enjoy his eclectic, upbeat, tender music. Lennon and Harrison borrowed, and were thought innovative, because people didn't always quite understand the borrowed material. McCartney made sure people did understand, and critics, understanding, scorned his work as derivative. Critics like to be a little uncertain. They like to think they need to work at it. Audiences, though, like to be charmed and delighted.

Crompton points out that Andrew Lloyd Webber has repeatedly taken shows where no show has gone before. In creating *Cats*, he drew from a literary source no one would have imagined. He approached it in a style no one would have expected of him, meeting the words just as they were, without changes. He and Trevor Nunn and Gillian Lynne and John Napier worked together to invent a style and form of theater—megamusical, "dance theater"—that had not been used in the West End or Broadway before. They did something new, but did it in a way that did not force the audience to wonder what the heck they were watching. Like McCartney, they made the new and unexpected accessible to anyone. *Cats*, and the many shows that followed, showed the professional centers of the theater world a new way to make a musical.

That blend of novelty and familiarity, of challenging material presented in emotional, accessible ways, goes a long way toward explaining why *Cats* was a megahit in 1981 and 1982, and why it continues to be a hit today. Andrew Lloyd Webber, like Paul McCartney, has the blessing and the curse of being an easily enjoyed innovator, and *Cats* remains an evergreen example of his virtues. Even in revival it retains a freshness and a charm that overrides all criticism, pleasing its audience and winning new fans.

DANCE MUSICAL

The use of dance is part of the spectacle of the megamusical. It's almost a hallmark at this point. The form includes massive dance, tells its story through dance, and is almost as dance-based as a ballet. In the style Gillian Lynne originated, the action is constant, expressive, energetic, and athletic. The megamusical depends on flashy dancing to keep the audience mesmerized. Viewers are moved as much by amazement as by empathy. Such high leaps! Such complicated movements!

Combined with a costuming style that also drew more from athletic and balletic norms than theater norms, the new approach changed how choreographers and directors thought about building a show. Older styles of musical focused on words and music. Dance, while important, was more decoration than storytelling. The story was told with words—words in songs, and words in spoken lines. The dances were an afterthought.

After *Cats*, and a few other outstanding dance musicals, *A Chorus Line* in particular, dance became a primary way of keeping the audience alert and engaged in the story. The approach was a blend of two major styles: the Vegas/Ice Capades show, and the ballet.

The Vegas/Ice Capades tradition was just short of circus: it was spectacular, gaudy, and athletic. The point of these shows was to amaze the audience with the power and energy of the dancing or skating. Even when a story was imposed on the show, it was seldom the point of the production. The point was razzle-dazzle and amazement.

The ballet seems the most likely source of the storytelling, though. Gillian Lynne was and is a ballet dancer herself, and had spent over a decade previous to *Cats* as a choreographer for various ballet productions. Ballet is not always about story, but it remains a storytelling form.

The combination of blatant, cheer-generating, razzle-dazzle with ballet narrative and acting skill made *Cats* possible. Much of the story and the audience attention depends on the dancers.

Once Broadway pros saw the new style, they ran with it. Modern musical theater remains more dance-oriented and athletic than the Golden Age style of dance. The former style counted on a show-stopping song. Now there's also the hope of a show-stopping dance that will get a standing ovation.

It's hard sometimes to remember that, at the time *Cats* opened, many people thought musical theater was dying. The Golden Age formulas and style seemed to have no place in a rock-and-roll age. Composers and choreographers seemed to know what to do with jazz, but not with the rock anthems and ballads of a new era. The emotional certainty of the old love stories no longer rang true. Those taking theater courses at the time were reading professional articles on the impending demise of popular musicals, leaving only the weak and limited audience for ballet, modern dance, and opera. Singers might hope for a place in the recording industry of the time. Dancers had almost no hope of a career.

That turned around when megamusicals became popular. It is once again a good strategy for a theater hopeful to have dance and singing skills to offer, along with dramatic training. Choreographers can hope for a professional career outside teaching.

Cats, as much as any show, helped establish that change. Andrew Lloyd Webber's brilliant ability to use any style of music to suit his needs brought a new sound into the theater. His need for a way to tell a story that did not depend entirely on words, though, brought him to collaborate with Gillian Lynne, and it was her ballet intuition that changed how theater used dance. Nothing has been the same since.

ANGELS American slang for people who invest in a show.

BOOK The word "book" means something different in theater, where it means the written words of a show, as opposed to any other portion of the performed material.

BROADWAY A central street in downtown Manhattan, in New York City. Many of New York's most famous and lucrative theaters are located on Broadway.

CHOREOGRAPHER An artist who creates dance, just as a writer creates a written work, and a composer creates a musical work.

CLOUD FUNDING The modern technique of funding a large project using many small-scale investors.

FRANCHISE A business term originating in models of marketing similar to that of the early McDonalds or Dairy Queen restaurants.

GOLDEN AGE MUSICAL The Golden Age of musical theater generally means the period between 1943 and 1959.

IMMERSIVE DESIGN A theater design intended to provide an entire world an audience can be involved in.

LITERARY EXECUTOR A person legally appointed to manage and protect an author's work after the author dies.

LYRICIST A person who writes the song lyrics for a single song or an entire musical.

MEGAMUSICAL A spectacular stage musical designed to awe and impress audiences with the experience of attending, rather than seduce them with a story.

MUSICAL In common theater terms, "a musical" is a long dramatic work built around songs which are used to present character development, emotional arcs, or plot points.

OFF-BROADWAY A broad term that usually means a theater production in or near New York City, but not on Broadway or in any of the major theaters associated with Broadway.

ORCHESTRA PIT A sunken, usually half-moon shaped, area at the foot of the stage, usually reserved for the orchestra that accompanies a musical production.

PASTICHE Art which copies the style and tone of a prior work or group of works.

PRODUCER A producer takes care of financial and business-oriented work in bringing a show to the stage.

PROSCENIUM STAGE The most common style of theatrical stage in Western culture. The stage is built at the front of the audience seating, set into a wall. The performance area is framed by an arch, and space on either side is hidden behind the walls of the arch, creating the wings.

REVUE A revue is similar to a collection of freestanding short stories. Most revues are built around songs, dance numbers, and short skits, with no central story to unify the material.

SCORE The music of a musical, including the music written for the orchestra as well as for the singers.

SET DESIGN The complete plan for a show's stage area.

THEATER-IN-THE-ROUND A style of performance in which the main stage is entirely surrounded by audience seating.

THRUST STAGE Any configuration where the performance stage extends out into the same room as the audience seating.

TOURING SHOW A version of a production that can travel from location to location, and adapt to different theater spaces, while still giving a stable and reliable version of the original show.

TYPESCRIPT If a hand-written copy of a book is a manuscript, then a typewritten copy of a book is a typescript.

VARIETY SHOWS See "revue." A show including music, dance, and comic skits, often with no connecting dramatic frame.

WEST END The British equivalent of Broadway.

Further Information

BOOKS

Coveney, Michael. *Cats on a Chandelier: The Andrew Lloyd Webber Story.*, London: Hutchinson, 1999.

Hanan, Stephen. *A Cat's Diary: How The Broadway Production of Cats Was Born.* Art of Theater. Hanover, NH: Smith and Kraus, 2002.

VIDEOS

Andrew Lloyd Webber—Trevor Nunn—Gillian Lynne, interview 2014

https://www.youtube.com/watch?v=_m3NqP5gvnQ.

At a press event before the London revival of the show, the show's original creative team shares their plans for the update.

Cats—Jellicle Songs for Jellicle Cats—Gillian Lynne vs. Andy Blankenbuehler's choreography

https://www.youtube.com/watch?v=5QhW5FAOtIs.

In split-screen format, this video compares the original show's choreography to that of the newer Broadway version.

The Naming of the Cats

https://www.youtube.com/watch?v=j7uTcYvoEbU&list
=PL7506A5ABABB2E025.

Taken from the 1998 film of the West End production, in this song, the ensemble introduces each character.

WEBSITES

Cats the Musical – Official Website and Tickets

https://www.catsthemusical.com

This site provides information on the history of the show, as well as where it is currently playing and how to buy tickets.

Bibliography

Bush, Ronald. "T. S. Eliot's Life and Career." Modern American Poetry (October 16, 2017), http://www. english.illinois.edu/maps/poets/a_f/eliot/life.htm

Compton, Sarah. "Why Lloyd Webber changed everything." *Telegraph*, May 8, 2002. http://www.telegraph.co.uk/ culture/theatre/drama/3577081/Why-Lloyd-Webber-changed-everything.html

Cox, Gordon. "'Cats': 5 Ways the Smash Musical Changed Broadway." *Variety*, August 2, 2012. http:// variety.com/2016/legit/news/how-cats-changed-broadway-1201827574

Eliot, Valerie. "Apropos of *Practical Cats*." TSEliot.com (October 16, 2017), http://tseliot.com/editorials/ reception-old-possums-book-of-practical-cats

Fowler, Rebecca. "How 'Cats' conquered the world." *Independent*, January 30, 1996. http://www.independent. co.uk/news/how-cats-conquered-the-world-1326547.html

"Letters from T. S. Eliot to the Tandy Family, with drafts of his cat poems." British Library (October 16, 2017), https://www.bl.uk/collection-items/letters-from-t-s-eliot-to-the-tandy-family-with-drafts-of-his-cat-poems

Lloyd Webber, Andrew. "T. S. Eliot and the inspiration behind Cats: A note from Andrew Lloyd Webber." The Really Useful Group, January 1, 1981. http://www.reallyuseful.com/show-blogs/t-s-eliot-and-the-inspiration-behind-cats

Mullan, John. "Style Council." *Guardian*, September 24, 2004. https://www.theguardian.com/books/2004/sep/25/classics.thomasstearnseliot

Rich, Frank. "Theater: Lloyd Webber's 'Cats.'" *New York Times*, October 8, 1982. http://www.nytimes.com/1982/10/08/theater/theater-lloyd-webber-s-cats.html?pagewanted=all&mcubz=0

Ricks, Christopher and Jim McClue, eds. *The Poems of T. S. Eliot Volume II: Practical Cats and Further Verses*. London: Faber & Faber, 2015

Riedel, Michael. "How 'Cats' was purrfected." *New York Post*, November 21, 2012. http://nypost.com/2012/11/21/how-cats-was-purrfected

Rothstein, Mervyn. "For 'Cats,' Nine Is The One To Celebrate." *New York Times*, October 7, 1991. http://www.nytimes.com/1991/10/07/theater/for-cats-nine-is-the-one-to-celebrate.html?mcubz=0

"Spotlight on T. S. Eliot." *Cats*, the Musical website (October 16, 2017), https://www.catsthemusical.com/now-and-forever/spotlight-on-ts-eliot

Sutherland, John. "An Introduction to *Old Possum's Book of Practical Cats*." British Library, May 25, 2016. https://www.bl.uk/20th-century-literature/articles/an-introduction-to-old-possums-book-of-practical-cats

Symonds, Dominic, and Millie Taylor. *Gestures of Music Theater: The Performativity of Song and Dance*. London: Oxford University Press, 2014

Walsh, Michael. "The Curiosity of Cats." *Smithsonian*, October 2007. http://www.smithsonianmag.com/arts-culture/the-curiosity-of-cats-164043365

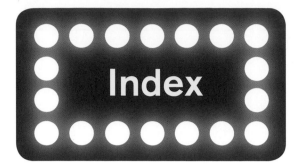

Index

Page numbers in **boldface** are illustrations.

About the Author

PEG ROBINSON is a writer and editor specializing in researched educational materials and white papers. She graduated from the University of California at Santa Barbara in 2008, with honors, and attended Pacifica Graduate Institution. She served for two years as a docent for Opus Archives, focusing on converting historically significant audio recordings to digital format, securing valuable material in a less fragile recording medium. She lives in Rhode Island, with her daughter and her cat and dog.